BEAVER POND
MOOSE POND

By Jim Arnosky

NATIONAL GEOGRAPHIC SOCIETY
Washington, D.C.

Published by the
National Geographic Society
1145 17th Street N.W.
Washington, D.C. 20036-4688

To create his paintings Jim Arnosky
used acrylics in an opaque oil technique
on bristol board.

Book design by Dorrit Green

The text of this book is set in Papyrus and Allise.

ISBN: ISBN 0-7922-7692-2

Printed in the U.S.A.

For Peter and Barbara

Let me take you to the mountains, to a very special place, where for one whole day a beaver pond became a moose pond too!

It was early in the morning.
Beaver had been up all night,
adding more sticks and mud to
his dam. A higher dam held more
water in the pond. And that is
what the beaver liked.

The pond was his—every inch of depth, every ripple in the water. Every bit of flooded meadow the beaver treated as his own. But to the other animals, it wasn't beaver's pond.

To the heron, who each morning watched
the beaver retire to his lodge, the pond
was a favorite place to fish and perch.
It was the perfect heron pond.

To the goldeneyes, it was a great duck pond, where they could drop in for a swim.

And to the young bull moose, it was a place for moose to drink and wade and eat green water plants. It was a MOOSE pond.

A cow moose led her calf out of the forest.
Mother moose was wary of the bull out in
the water. She and her calf lingered at the
water's edge. Then something in the nearby
woods made a grunting noise.

It was the biggest bull moose
in the forest! The great big bull
moose snorted loudly at the cow and calf,
warning them to go away.

Mother moose led her calf into the pond.

The smaller bull was still feeding in the water. The wary cow moose kept the beaver's lodge between them.

The calf liked being in the pond. He knew how to swim. He swam all afternoon just for fun. And later in the day, he swam in deeper water to escape the swarms of biting flies.

When the sun was setting, the calf watched the evening swallows fly. Then at dusk, he and his mother left the pond to bed down in the woods. The young bull moose left also.

The big old bull had the whole pond to himself. That is, until he saw the beaver swimming, rested and ready for another busy night. The bull moose grunted loudly at the beaver. MOOSE POND! But the beaver would not go away. BEAVER POND!

Moose and beaver shared
the pond, each waiting for
the other one to leave.

Then finally, it was the moose who slowly walked away. The beaver stayed. It was the beaver's pond—every bit of flooded meadow, every inch of depth, and every ripple in the water.

Beavers are clumsy on land but agile in water. They create ponds by damming streams so they can swim, not walk, to their food source, which is the surrounding brush. The beaver's instinctive impulse to flood an area of food benefits many other animals. The pond becomes a habitat for aquatic insects, amphibians, fish, birds, other mammals, and more.

This book shows the beaver as an unwitting yet magnificent provider for other wildlife. I want the children to see how a beaver pond can be a duck pond, frog pond, heron pond, trout pond, and moose pond all at once. More important, I want

children to begin to understand how each of
these animals utilizes and regards the pond
as its own special place, while the pond remains
essentially the beaver's domain.

Beaver Pond, Moose Pond can be used to spark
discussion about shared habitat and coexistence
in the wild.

Jim Arnosky

www.jimarnosky.com

The world's largest nonprofit scientific and educational organization,
the National Geographic Society was founded in 1888
"for the increase and diffusion of geographic knowledge." Since then
it has supported scientific exploration and spread information to its
more than nine million members worldwide.

The National Geographic Society educates and inspires millions
every day through magazines, books, television programs, videos, maps
and atlases, research grants, the National Geographic Bee, teacher
workshops, and innovative classroom materials.

The Society is supported through membership dues and income from the
sale of its educational products. Members receive NATIONAL GEOGRAPHIC
magazine–the Society's official journal–discounts on Society products,
and other benefits.

For more information about the National Geographic Society and
its educational programs and publications, please call
1-800-NGS-LINE (647-5463),
or write to the following address:

National Geographic Society
1145 17th Street N.W.
Washington, D.C. 20036-4688 U.S.A.

Visit the Society's Web site: www.nationalgeographic.com